# Animal Blessings

# Also by June Cotner

*Bedside Prayers*

*Bless the Day*

*Family Celebrations*

*Get Well Wishes*

*Graces*

*Heal Your Soul, Heal the World*

*The Home Design Handbook*

# Animal Blessings

## Prayers and Poems Celebrating Our Pets

JUNE COTNER

HarperSanFrancisco
*A Division of* HarperCollins*Publishers*

**The author is donating a portion of the proceeds from**
***Animal Blessings*** **to benefit animal welfare organizations.**

FIRST EDITION

*Designed by Jessica Shatan*

Library of Congress Cataloging-in-Publication Data

Cotner, June
    Animal Blessings: prayers and poems celebrating our pets / June Cotner.
    —1st ed.
        p. cm.
    Includes index.
    ISBN 0–06–251645–0 (cloth)
        1. Human-animal relationships—Religious aspects. 2. Pet owners—
    Prayer-books and devotions—English. 3. Human-animal relationships—
    Poetry. 4. English poetry. I. Title
    BL439 .C67 2000
    291.4'32—dc21                                                    00-039523

00 01 02 03 04 FG 10 9 8 7 6 5 4 3 2

For all the dear animals who have shared
their hearts with me and allowed me
the pleasure of their company

*Pretty Peatie Boy*
*Mickey*
*Pixie*
*Sundance*
*Shalimar*
*Peaches*
*Cali*
*Thunder*
*Spree*
*Tora*
*Kiki*
*Charlie*
*Mary*
*Allante*
*Mr. Tabby*

# Contents

## ONE Dogs 1

## TWO Cats 27

# THREE Other Animals 51

# FOUR Partings 85

# FIVE Reflections 107

# SIX Inspiration 145

# A Letter to Readers

I write this letter as our dogs, Allante and Mary, sit a few feet from me sleeping by the fire; Mr. Tabby, our cat, is snoozing on the coffee table directly in front of me, occasionally making his way onto my pad of writing paper; and our other cat, Kiki, is curled up on the back of the sofa next to my shoulders. I consider them my guardian angels, these precious animals who have found their way to our home. They surround me with affection, are concerned for my well-being, and keep their watchful guard. When I gaze into their eyes, they each look back with the utmost kindness, love, and serenity. They're a calming presence in my life and a never-depleted source of love. As my teachers they have taught me that there is joy in simplicity, that laughter should be a daily exercise, and that words aren't necessary to communicate love.

When you add a pet to your family, you never know what's ahead. We've had Sundance, who loved to sneak chicken off the BBQ; Thunder, our German shepherd, who always slept under my feet in the office and followed me wherever I went as if to convey, "At your service, ma'am"; Shalimar who gave the best "dog" hug to cheer me up; Peaches, our golden retriever, who was inseparable from Cali, our white cat (both shown on the title page); Mr. Tabby, our stray cat who can "sit and shake" on cue (for a treat, of course!); and Kiki, who came to us as a wild cat and is now almost a lap cat, almost.

We're now into our "third" generation of animals. I never thought of it that way until I overheard a man remark that his parents were now into their third generation of dogs. I thought, "Third generation? Yup, that's me."

My friend, Sandi Dahlquist, shared the essence of a lovely quote with me—that it takes a special person to love a pet knowing in all likelihood that the person will outlive the animal, and therefore must experience the heartbreaking pain of their passing. Sandi went on to comment that for a lifelong animal lover advancing in age, the choice of whether to take in an animal becomes more complicated when the question becomes, "Will my pet outlive me?" Her comment made me realize that regardless of whether we're young or old, it's important to arrange for a guardian for our pets and provisions for them in our wills. Should the unexpected happen, our grieving pets will be lost without us; we don't need to compound their misery by having our "family" members abandoned at a shelter.

I've been creating poetry anthologies for a number of years now. In my heart, I knew that *Animal Blessings* would be one of my most important books. I wanted to find a way to honor all animals, both in our homes and in the wild, who bring immeasurable joy to our lives. I hope I have succeeded. Since animals do not have voices, I hope this book will become their voice and our "call" to create better living situations for all animals on our planet. Most of all, I want *Animal Blessings* to honor the profound influence all animals make in our lives.

I hope that you, too, are surrounded by the blessings of animals. I sincerely believe that pets add a special quality to life that can't be measured. I know this. Some of my dearest friends in life have been cats and dogs.

—JUNE COTNER
P.O. Box 2765
Poulsbo, WA 98370
june@junecotner.com
www.junecotner.com

*A Letter to Readers*

# Thanks

*Animal Blessings* would not have become a reality without the love my animals have given me throughout my life. The book grew out of a passion to find a way to celebrate, honor, and dignify my deep respect for the blessings that animals bring to all of our lives.

But it takes a lot more than love and passion to bring a book to fruition. I'm deeply grateful for my dear friend and hard-working agent, Denise Marcil, who was immediately excited about *Animal Blessings* when I first mentioned it to her about five years ago. I credit Denise with creating what has now become my full-time career: creating and editing inspirational poetry anthologies.

Harper San Francisco is the perfect publisher for *Animal Blessings.* I continue to learn much from their expertise, dedication to excellence, and I appreciate their commitment to publishing spiritual books. In particular, I'd like to thank Steve Hanselman, vice president and associate publisher; Terri K. Leonard, senior managing editor; Liz Perle, editor-at-large; David Hennessy, associate editor; Margery Buchanan, marketing director; Kathi Goldmark, associate marketing and publicity director; Eric Brandt, publicist; and a highly creative book jacket designer, Jim Warner.

I'm deeply grateful for my talented assistants in the office: Cheryl Edmonson (book production and overall office management), Rebecca Pirtle (obtaining permissions and setting up my book events), Virginia Donald (typing, filing, and errands), and Gemma Arcangel (mailings). Others in the local community have extended themselves in the creation of my books. Specifically, the staff at both the Poulsbo and Kingston libraries have obtained a number of reference books for me; Suzanne Droppert, owner of Liberty Bay Books, gives me continual feedback at each stage of a book's production; and Kevin Jennings, computer consultant, brings good cheer my way as he helps me with my sometime errant computer.

*Animal Blessings* would not have become the book it has without the inclusion of outstanding, heartfelt poems from poets who have contributed to my anthologies for many years now. Thank you so much for your treasured words! You should be pleased to know that your poem survived the scrutiny of my review of over 3,000 submissions.

Then, after I selected my favorites, my "test market" panel gave me their specific feedback on which poems should be in the book. Specifically, for providing a careful critique, I'd like to thank editor David Hennessy, intern Alex Kasavin (both of Harper San Francisco), and editor Joyce Standish (who has her own editing company in Las Vegas, "papers").

To ensure that my selections were appealing to those of various beliefs, I'm deeply grateful to Father Paul Keenan (author of *Good News for Bad Days* and *Stages of the Soul*, cohost of the national ABC radio program "Religion on the Line," and host of "As You Think"); Rabbi Rami M. Shapiro (storyteller, poet, and author of *The Way of Solomon* and five other books); and Reverend Gary W. Huffman (coauthor of *The Bible: A to Z* and pastor of First Presbyterian Church, PCUSA, Shelbyville, Indiana).

Representing the veterinary perspective, I'd like to thank Deanna Middaugh, who is the wife of my veterinarian, and long-time friend, Alisa Huckell, who is now in veterinary school.

I'd like to express a very warm thank-you to the following poets who lent their expertise to this book and gave me a careful critique: Barbara Crooker (prolific poet who has been published in five of my anthologies and winner of many poetry awards), Susan J. Erickson (a talented, "late bloomer" poet who started writing at age 55 and was published in *Bless the Day, Family Celebrations*, and this book), Margaret Ann Huffman (award-winning journalist, author of *Through the Valley: Prayers for Violent Times* and twenty-nine other books), Arlene Gay Levine (author of *39 Ways to Open Your Heart* and published in six of my anthologies), Donna Wahlert (award-winning poet and contributor to *Heal Your Soul, Heal the World* and this book), Barbara Younger (author of

*Thanks*

———

*xxii*

*Purple Mountain Majesties: The Story of Katharine Lee Bates and "America the Beautiful"*), and her daughter, Katherine Younger.

Rounding out the perspective in helping me make the final selections for *Animal Blessings*, I'd like to thank the following animal lovers: my husband and best friend, Jim Graves; my hiking buddy and cat fanatic, Wendy McClure (she once took in ten stray cats and is now down to "only" four); my employees, Cheryl Edmonson, Rebecca Pirtle, Lacey Menne, and Virginia Donald; and dear friends, Sue Peterson, Patricia Huckell, Virginia Lynn Bradley, Sue Gitch, Joanie Guggenmos, and Jenny-Marie Pulliam.

I'm ever so thankful for my children, Kyle and Kirsten Myrvang, who have brought tremendous joy to my life as well the pleasure of shared memories of all of our relationships with our pets over the years.

And last, I'm grateful to God for bringing the blessings of animals to our world.

# ONE

# Dogs

## What I Learned from My Dog

Never pass up the opportunity to go for a joyride.
Allow the experience of fresh air and the wind in my
    face to be pure ecstasy.
When loved ones come home, I will always run to
    greet them.
Let others know when they have invaded my
    territory.
Take naps and stretch before rising.
Run, romp, and play daily.
Eat with gusto and enthusiasm.
Be loyal.
Never pretend to be something I am not.
If what I want lies buried, I will dig until I find it.
When someone is having a bad day, I will be silent,
    sit close by, and nuzzle him gently.
Thrive on attention, and let people touch you.
Avoid biting when a simple growl will do.
On hot days, drink lots of water and lie under a
    shady tree.
When you're happy, dance around and wag your
    entire body.

**Dogs**

No matter how often one is scolded, don't buy into the guilt thing and pout—run back and make friends.

Delight in the simple joy of a long walk.

AUTHOR UNKNOWN

*Dogs*

## I Would Be

I'd be an ungainly half-grown Labrador
In the Lord's House,
Slipping through an unnoticed side door,
Knocking the black hymnals off the pews.

And He would call me by my secret name.

There I would be quivering,
Not knowing anything,
Understanding nothing
But the sound
In that voice.

Forgiven the muddy carpet
The kneeling pad chewed up in waiting.

Strung taut with joy,
No mind, no thought, just the sheer pull of it,
His voice, and I'd leap into it,
A hoop of gold.

JANET McCANN

**Dogs**

5

## Welcome Home, New Puppy

May I be worthy, God of new beginnings, of this wee one trotting in my wake. I'm already in love with this wriggly ball of fur with milky puppy breath, needle teeth as sharp as exclamation points, growls that sound like bees buzzing, and bright button eyes that've taken my measure in a heartbeat and know me for the infatuated fool I am. Bless us as we explore the world You've set before us. Down on my knees in the wake of a puppy, O God, is a wonderful place to meet You.

MARGARET ANNE HUFFMAN

*Dogs*

## Making a House a Home

For me a house or an apartment becomes a home when you add one set of four legs, a happy tail, and that indescribable measure of love we call a dog.

ROGER CARAS
President *Emeritus* of the American Society for the Prevention of Cruelty to Animals

*Dogs*

7

## Faithful Companion

I have come to expect
his eager cries
as he looks out
into the snowy February night,
under the valentine moon
that shines
and sparkles and glitters
on the snowy banks.

He streaks
into the diamond night
across the slippery deck.
He flies over the edge
past crocuses, daffodils, and forsythia.

I have come to expect
the sound of his ferocious voice
as he protects his family.
He returns.

*Dogs*

I hear the scratching at the door.
I feel his icy kiss.

I have come to expect him.

KATY FRIENDS, AGE 12

*Dogs*

## Just My Dog

He's just my dog.

He is my other eyes that can see above the clouds, my other ears that hear above the winds. He is the part of me that can reach out to sea.

He has told me a thousand times over that I am his reason for being—by the way he rests against my leg; by the way he thumps his tail at my smallest smile; by the way he shows his hurt when I leave without taking him—I think it makes him sick with worry when he is not along to care for me.

When I am wrong, he is delighted to forgive. When I am angry, he clowns to make me smile. When I am happy, he is joy unbounded.

When I am a fool, he ignores it. When I succeed, he brags.

Without him, I am only another man. With him, I am all-powerful.

He is loyalty itself. He has taught me the meaning of devotion.

With him, I know a secret comfort and a private

*Dogs*

10

peace. He has brought me understanding where before I was ignorant.

His head on my knee can heal human hurts. His presence by my side is protection against my fears of dark and unknown things. He has promised to wait for me—whenever, wherever—in case I need him. And I expect I will, as I always have.

He's just my dog.

GENE HILL

*Dogs*

## We Really Never Own a Dog

I used to think, with pride overflowing, that my brown dog was mine. Now I know better. We never really own a dog as much as he owns us. Where he led I would follow without fear, and even now, remembering how he would curl up with his back against my bedroom door, I know again how it was to feel safe and protected from anything and anyone.

Once when I was very small and sick my mother put him in bed with me against everyone's advice. "They need each other," she said, and that was that. She understood brown dogs and their peculiar magic.

GENE HILL

*Dogs*

## Loyal Friend

The one absolutely unselfish friend that man can have in this selfish world, the one that never deserts him, the one that never proves ungrateful or treacherous, is his dog. . . . When all other friends desert, he remains.

GEORGE GRAHAM VEST
From an 1884 speech to the United States Senate

***Dogs***

## A Perfect Gentleman

To call him a dog hardly seems to do him justice, though inasmuch as he had four legs, a tail and barked, I admit he was, to all outward appearances. But to those of us who knew him well, he was a perfect gentleman.

HERMIONE GINGOLD
(1897–1987)

*Dogs*

## Old Friends

Their youthful years have slipped away,
The old man and his dog.
They have a special bonding
That needs no dialogue.

The chase is just a memory,
But how they used to run
When hearts and legs were stronger
And games were such great fun.

Now the pace is slower
For the master and his mate.
If one lags too far behind
The other stops to wait.

Some things we cannot change
Like aging and the weather,
But true friends are quite content
Just growing old together.

C. DAVID HAY

*Dogs*

15

## Old Black Lab in the First Snow

The old black lab
prances through the stark cold,
head high, bound to fetch
the falling sky.

Snowflakes, dogstars of her youth,
drive her seasonally mad.
The hoary jowl unlocks the tail,
a marionette on dancing string.

Pup reborn
in the cataract of winter's eye,
she darts away and fails to grasp
old age, remembering.

JULIA OLDER

*Dogs*

## Scratch a Dog

Scratch a dog and you'll find a permanent job.

FRANKLIN P. JONES

***Dogs***

## Devotion

I have found that when you are deeply troubled there are things you get from the silent devoted companionship of a dog that you can get from no other source.

DORIS DAY

*Dogs*

## Comfort

I, who had had my heart full for hours, took advantage of an early moment of solitude, to cry in it very bitterly. Suddenly a little hairy head thrust itself from behind my pillow into my face, rubbing its ears and nose against me in a responsive agitation, and drying the tears as they came.

ELIZABETH BARRETT BROWNING
(1806–1861)

**Dogs**

19

## A Dog's Prayer

Treat me kindly, my beloved master, for no heart in all the world is more grateful for kindness than the loving heart of me.

Do not break my spirit with a stick, for though I should lick your hand between the blows, your patience and understanding will more quickly teach me the things you would have me do.

Speak to me often, for your voice is the world's sweetest music, as you must know by the fierce wagging of my tail when your footstep falls upon my waiting ear.

When it is cold and wet, please take me inside, for I am now a domesticated animal, no longer used to bitter elements. And I ask no greater glory than the privilege of sitting at your feet beside the hearth. Though had you no home, I would rather follow you through ice and snow than rest upon the softest pillow in the warmest home in all the land, for you are my god and I am your devoted worshiper.

Keep my pan filled with fresh water, for although I should not reproach you were it dry, I cannot tell you

*Dogs*

when I suffer thirst. Feed me clean food, that I may stay well, to romp and play and do your bidding, to walk by your side, and stand ready, willing and able to protect you with my life should your life be in danger.

And, beloved master, should the great Master see fit to deprive me of my health or sight, do not turn me away from you. Rather hold me gently in your arms as skilled hands grant me the merciful boon of eternal rest—and I will leave you knowing with the last breath I drew, my fate was ever safest in your hands.

BETH NORMAN HARRIS

*Dogs*

## Folks Will Know

Folks will know how large your soul is
by the way you treat a dog.

CHARLES F. DURAN

**Dogs**

# A Dog's Acceptance

Say something idiotic
and nobody but a dog politely wags his tail.

VIRGINIA GRAHAM

**Dogs**

## If You Can

If you can start the day without caffeine,
If you can get going without pep pills,
If you can resist complaining and boring people with
    your troubles,
If you can eat the same food every day and be
    grateful for it,
If you can understand when your loved ones are too
    busy to give you any time,
If you can overlook it when something goes wrong
    through no fault of yours and those you love
    take it out on you,
If you can take criticism and blame without
    resentment,
If you can ignore a friend's limited education and
    never correct him,
If you can resist treating a rich friend better than a
    poor friend,
If you can face the world without lies and deceit,
If you can conquer tension without medical help,
If you can relax without liquor,
If you can sleep without the aid of drugs,

If you can honestly say that deep in your heart you
    have no prejudice against creed, color, religion,
    or politics,
Then, my friends, you are almost as good as your dog.

AUTHOR UNKNOWN

*Dogs*

# Cats

## Cats Make Us Feel Good

Cats make one of the most satisfying sounds in the world: they purr. Almost all cats make us feel good about ourselves because they let us know they feel good about us, about themselves, and about our relationship with them. A purring cat is a form of high praise, like a gold star on a test paper. It is reinforcement we would all like to believe about ourselves— that we are nice.

ROGER CARAS
President *Emeritus* of the American Society for the Prevention of Cruelty to Animals

**Cats**

## Magician

Then my best friend
on all the Earth
sits upon my lap
not to be comforted
but to soothe

Wizard of the heart,
my cat,
when the world fails
or the day weighs,
with a wave of the tail
or soulful glance
makes the Universe
shine once more

ARLENE GAY LEVINE

*Cats*

## Peace Keeper

As I lie in the state between
Sleep and consciousness,
I feel the nudge of your head,
More insistent the second time,
Until my hand rises and you gently glide under.

Your whiskers tickle my wrist,
My hand enjoys the cool silkiness of your fur,
As you saunter past
To settle against the curve of my legs,
Then ever so quietly, methodically, you begin to purr.

"Sweet dreams," I breathe . . .
To the keeper of my peace and contentment
As we both . . . finally,
Drift off to sleep.

MARY MAUDE DANIELS

**Cats**

## Time Spent Watching a Cat

is not deducted
from your span on Earth.

RICHARD BEBAN

**Cats**

## The Difference Between Dogs and Cats

A dog thinks: Hey, these people I live with feed me, love me, provide me with a nice warm, dry house, pet me, and take good care of me . . . they must be Gods!

A cat thinks: Hey, these people I live with feed me, love me, provide me with a nice warm, dry house, pet me, and take good care of me . . . I must be a God!

AUTHOR UNKNOWN

**Cats**

## Basic Rules for Cats Who Have a House to Run

### Doors

- Do not allow closed doors in any room. To get a door opened, stand on your hind legs and hammer with your forepaws (screaming like you are being injured helps, too). Once the door is opened, it is not necessary to use it. After you have ordered an outside door opened, stand halfway out and think about several things. This is particularly important during very cold weather, rain, snow, and mosquito season.

### Guests

- Quickly determine which guest hates cats the most. Sit on that lap. If you can manage to have Friskies Fish 'n' Glop on your breath, so much the better.

- For sitting on laps or rubbing against trouser legs, select a fabric color that contrasts well with your

Cats

fur. For example, white furred cats go to black wool clothing.

- When walking among dishes on the dinner table, be prepared to look surprised and hurt when scolded. The idea is to convey: "But you allow me on the table when company is not here."

- Always accompany guests to the bathroom. It is not necessary to do anything, just sit and stare.

## Work

- If one of your humans is sewing or knitting or writing and another one is idle, stay with the busy one. This is called helping, otherwise known as hampering.

- For book readers, get in close under the chin, between the eyes and the book (unless you can lie across the book itself).

*Cats*

- When supervising cooking, sit just behind the left heel of the cook. You cannot be seen and thereby stand a better chance of being stepped on and picked up and consoled.

**Play**

- It is important. Get enough sleep during the daytime so that you are fresh for playing catch-mouse or king-of-the-hill on your human's bed between 2:00 and 4:00 A.M.

*Begin people training early. You will then have a smooth-running household. Humans need to know the basic rules. They can be taught if you start early and are consistent.*

AUTHOR UNKNOWN

**Cats**

## The Cat

Aloof, detached, she calmly stands
ignoring my calls, my outstretched hands.
And that's when I know and am sure as can be
that I don't own her. She really owns me.
At times she's content asleep on my lap
full of affection taking her nap.
But just when I think I know that soft head,
she changes her mind and wants freedom instead.
So I say, "I'll ignore her. I'll ignore her small cries."
But she knows she can change me with her deep
	pleading eyes.
Yet she never is guilty. She never has shame.
I'm always the problem. I'm always to blame.
But perhaps there is wisdom in her strange, changing
	ways,
a message profound that she calmly displays.
Perhaps we live together and are more fully
	contented,
when we appreciate each other and take less for
	granted.

THOMAS L. REID

Cats

## Psalm for a Cat Owner

I am your servant. You shall not want.
You maketh me to lie down where cat hair abounds.
You leadeth me to pricey pet stores for toys and trinkets
      to amuse and adorn your inner kitten.
You guideth me to sunny spots for afternoon naps.
Yea, even though you walk on the kitchen counters,
      fear neither rod nor staff, for thou art
      my heart's meow.
I prepareth a feast before you to tempt your
      capricious appetite.
I brush your coat with gentle strokes.
I dispose of your repugnant hairballs with practiced
      aplomb.
My indulgence overfloweth.
Surely warmth and purring shall follow you all
      the days of your nine lives
and we will dwell in mutual affection in the house
      that once was mine.

Cats

SUSAN J. ERICKSON

*Companion*

Is there anything more satisfying
on a cold, blustery day,
Than a good book,
A hearty fire,
And a soft purring friend by your side?

MARY MAUDE DANIELS

**Cats**

## The King of Cats Sends a Postcard to His Wife

Keep your whiskers crisp and clean.
Do not let the mice grow lean.
Do not let yourself grow fat
like a common kitchen cat.

Have you set the kittens free?
Do they sometimes ask for me?
Is our catnip growing tall?
Did you patch the garden wall?

Clouds are gentle walls that hide
gardens on the other side.
Tell the tabby cats I take
all my meals with William Blake,

lunch at noon and tea at four,
served in splendor on the shore
at the tinkling of a bell.
Tell them I am sleeping well.

**Cats**

NANCY WILLARD

# On a Cat, Aging

He blinks upon the hearth rug,
And yawns in deep content,
Accepting all the comforts
That Providence has sent.

Louder he purrs, and louder,
In one glad hymn of praise
For all the night's adventures,
For quiet restful days.

Life will go on forever,
With all that cat can wish,
Warmth and the glad procession
of fish and milk and fish.

Only—the thought disturbs him—
He's noticed once or twice,
The times are somehow breeding
A nimbler race of mice.

SIR ALEXANDER GRAY
(1882–1968)

*Cats*

## Room for One More

Thank you for my cat, O God. A little worn around her edges and frayed about the ears, she's a beauty nonetheless, our Orphan Annie Cat. She never speaks of her previous lives, choosing to shroud herself in mystery as she twines about our feet and into our hearts. I think of her as an adventuresome hobo, or perhaps a traveling circus star, or famous actress in disguise. Whatever the truth, winding up here for her encore, she and I agree, was a match made in Heaven.

MARGARET ANNE HUFFMAN

*Cats*

## Cat from the Animal Shelter

Old, lost, gaunt, frightened,
you were no barn cat.
Dignified as a dowager,
your craving for chicken scraps and fat
declared you once belonged,
were somebody's pampered house pet.

With your unkempt black beauty and trustful
    affection,
not fawning, but as appealing as a good dog's,
you cheated death. They pronounced you
much too nice to destroy,
said they couldn't put you down.

After her husband's sudden death,
she took you home, gave you shelter,
held tight your large, bony, tense softness
all night and wondered in the morning
whether she saved you
or you saved her.

KATHLEEN McKINLEY HARRIS

**Cats**

## Cat-Haiku-Esque-Poem

It's nice to see a cat curled up
with a good book. Sadly it is
the book I want to read.

Ÿ. MAX VALENTONIS

**Cats**

## I Will Always Remember

I will always remember
the olive-eyed tabby who
taught me that not all
relationships are meant to
last a lifetime. Sometimes
just an hour is enough to
touch your heart.

BARBARA L. DIAMOND

*Cats*

## Passerby

A pure white cat with pink ears
I never saw before in my backyard
looks at me calmly
as I stamp and shush
and sting my hands clapping her off.
In her own time
she starts away and moves in mystery
and dignity. What if
the trespasser were an angel?
Would I say I didn't like cats then?
If I want the best in everything
doesn't that call for my best?
The floating walk, the sprightly carriage
speak authority; the absence
of a collar, available.
She turns to look back—only once,
in her eyes a curiosity, a gentleness,
utterly without recrimination.
I think of the hollow ring in my house
as I walk through the rooms.

Cats

In a surge of feeling I call to her.
She hesitates, then comes with a bound
as if she had heard the loving voice
many times before.

IDA FASEL

*Cats*

## A Question

When I play with my cat, who knows if I am not a pastime to her more than she is to me?

MONTAIGNE
(1533–1592)

**Cats**

## Stray Cat

Oh, what unhappy twist of fate
Has brought you homeless to my gate?
The gate where once another stood
To beg for shelter, warmth, and food
For from that day I ceased to be
The master of my destiny.

While he, with purr and velvet paw,
Became within my house the law.
He scratched the furniture and shed
And claimed the middle of my bed.

He ruled in arrogance and pride
And broke my heart the day he died.
So if you really think, oh Cat,
I'd willingly relive all that
Because you come forlorn and thin
Well . . . don't just stand there . . . Come on in!

FRANCIS WITHAM

*Cats*

## Cats as Teachers

We have learned many things from living with [our cats]. Some lessons are directives we would be wise to follow: Live a rhythmic life. Sit and savor the present moment. Gaze intently. Stretch often. Keep out of harm's way. Take good care of your family. Be independent, but don't be afraid of being dependent on others. Cherish your wildness, even if no one else does. When you want something, be persistent. When someone pays attention to you, respond with affection. If you are embarrassed, turn your back on the situation and get on with your life. Enjoy small treats. Keep yourself clean. Take a nap when you need one, and try to relax more.

FREDERIC AND MARY ANN BRUSSAT

**Cats**

# THREE

# Other Animals

# A Fieldmouse's Prayer

Keep strong, O Lord, our aged maple,
Rock it for us like a cradle;
When the wind begins to howl,
Hide us from the midnight owl.

Keep us from the sight of bats;
Soothe us with the sounds of gnats.
Save us from the bright green snakes
That crawl here from the nearby lakes.

Send instead the songs of crickets
Who sing so loudly from the thickets;
Bless for us the fireflies,
That wink at us like God's own eyes.

Save us from the floods of rain—
Protect our little store of grain.
Keep it from the warring ants
Who scorn the grasshopper's lifelong dance;

Guard us from the night's black yawn,
Keep us safely till the dawn—

Other Animals

And in the golden light of day
Bring a better world our way.

Nicolas Kallistos

*Other Animals*

## All God's Creatures

I have a habit of collecting the cast-off, unwanted, injured, lost, or otherwise unfortunate animals I come across. Since childhood I have been known to come home with lost kittens, unwanted dogs, orphaned birds, wounded snakes, malnourished lizards, lacerated horses, or any combination of the above. Some have died despite my efforts, others found aid with wildlife programs and were released, yet more were adopted by friends and family who had lost an animal of their own. A few have, through luck and circumstance, spent years with me.

Of all the animals, Einstein the Iguana is one of my favorites. Despite my family's initial protest, all of them now fondly remember her. Einstein came to us as the result of a compromise between my mother and me. I really wanted a snake; however, my mother refused to have something in the house that required live food. When I suggested a vegetarian lizard, she had no arguments left. We found Einstein in a small shop in Berkeley back when few people thought of iguanas as pets. She was on sale because she was

Other Animals

missing all but three of the trademark spines on her back. I fell in love with her instantly.

I could relay hours of stories about our adventures with Einstein. How our very male-acting lizard surprised all of us when "he" laid eggs and we had to re-evaluate "his" gender. How she used to walk around with the parakeet riding on her back, unconcerned with her talkative passenger. Her trip to Texas in our truck, sunning herself on the dashboard, and receiving stares from strangers who didn't believe she was actually alive. Life on the boat with her (if you ever need a good pet for a boat, I highly recommend an iguana). How she overcame her fear of dogs and would chase four full-size dogs out of the kitchen to beg for scraps of salmon. But the thing I am most often asked, is did she have a personality?

Of course, she did.

JENNY-MARIE PULLIAM

*Other Animals*

## Three Little Fish

Who would have thought, three fish in a bowl
Could teach so many of life's lessons
To a four-year-old.

Lessons of love, caring for another
Lessons of responsibility,
Of being their "mother."

Lessons of loss, that life does end
Lessons of heartache,
Of missing a friend.

Lessons of faith, of unending love
Lessons of trust
In Heaven above.

Three little fish, how did God know
Would teach so much
To a four-year-old.

CHERYL MORIKAWA

**Other Animals**

## Grace

Twilight begins
The embrace of stars.
I attend to softening edges,
Watch the unassuming beauty of
Horses as they bow their heads
Over sweet, sun-dried grasses.

This is the most peaceful time I know.
Paced by clover-scented, rhythmic chewing,
Content with present abundance
I slow the natural pulse
Of earth and sky

To simple needs—
Warm breath on hand,
Comfortable intimacy in serene eyes.
For it is the horse's gift
To connect us with heaven
And our own footsteps.

Each evening
I look forward to this transition,
This precious mystery of

Communion with the still Earth
As I gently slip out of this binding human skin
And dance with child-like grace before the
 setting sun.

RONNI SWEET

*Other Animals*

## A Pony's Prayer

I pray that gentle hands may guide my feet;
I ask for kind commands from voices sweet;
At night a stable warm with scented hay,
Where, safe from every harm, I'll sleep till day.

AUTHOR UNKNOWN

*Other Animals*

## Last Chance

It happened so sudden, twelve years in my past,
For the rest of my life the injury would last.
The cars hit head-on, not a chance to slow down,
The next I remember, I lay on the ground.
My hip joint was crushed beyond all repair,
"You're too young to replace it," Doc said with a
      stare.
"You'll walk again but you'll never run."
These words hit me hard like the shot from a gun.

Ten years came and went, the pain more severe.
I said to my wife, "Replacement time's here."
When the surgery was over, Doc said to my wife,
"He can't ride a horse for the rest of his life."
We own our own farm with a full riding stable,
So horses and riding put food on our table.
I could sell horses and tack, and some money I'd
      make,
But to ride one myself was a risk I couldn't take.

And then it did happen, one night at the sale,
As I stood selling halters inside of the rail.

*Other Animals*

My wife came to me with that look in her eye,
She said, "There's a horse out back ready to die."
As I walked to the pen and looked over the fence,
There stood a starved gelding whose frame was
     immense.
His eyes were three inches sunk back in his head,
If he were lying down, you would have sworn he was
     dead.
He stood sixteen-one, weighed about four and a
     quarter,
His hair was three inches and not one-half shorter.
A skeleton with hide stood before my own eyes,
If he walked through the ring, it would be a surprise.

As the barn door slid open and they led him on in,
The auctioneer said, "Two hundred is where we'll
     begin."
The kill buyer said, "Two-oh-five's all I'll give."
I said, "I'll give two-ten just to see if he'll live."
The bids then quit coming, not a sound from the
     crowd,
The next word was "Sold," he said very loud.

As the trailer backed up to the wood loading gate,
I said, "Let's get him home before it's too late."

He had to have help to step up to the floor,
But we got him in and then closed the door.
As I drove home that night, I looked back at a
       glance,
And said, "If he lives, we'll call him Last Chance."

Well, we made the trip home, and he lived through
       the night.
When the vet came next morning, he said, "What a
       sight."
We floated his teeth and trimmed all his feet,
Gave him wormer and thiamin and a little to eat.
My vet said his heart was as strong as a drum,
If we brought him "'long slowly" the rest may just
       come.

Well, his weight started coming and his health soon
       returned.
He showed us his love he must have thought we had
       earned.
He would whinny and nicker as I walked to the shed,
As if to say, "Thanks, 'cause of you, I'm not dead."
He would stroll the whole place without being
       penned,
He'd come when I called, just like man's best friend.

*Other Animals*

63

Three months had gone by since the night of the
    sale,
My wife had him tied on our old hitchin' rail.
I asked her, "What's up?" as I just came outside.
She said that "It's time to see if he'll ride."
She threw on the blanket, saddle, bridle and said,
"The worst that could happen, I'll get tossed on my
    head."
As her seat hit the leather, he stood like a rock.
With a tap of her heels, he started to walk.
He reined to the left and he reined to the right,
The bit in his mouth he sure didn't fight.
He did what she asked without second thought.
She cantered him on and not once he fought.
When she returned from the ride with a tear in
    her eye,
She said, "He's the one, would you like to try?"

I thought to myself as I stood at his side,
If this giant's that gentle, why not take a ride?
It had been a long time, but the look on his face
Said, "Hop on, my good friend, let's ride 'round this
    place."

We rode 'round the yard, then out through the gate,
This giant and me, it must have been fate.
He gave me back part of my life that I lost,
I knew then I'd keep him, no matter what cost.

I've been offered two thousand, and once even three,
But no money on earth would buy him from me.
You see, we share something special, this gelding
    and me,
A chance to start over, a chance to be free.
And when the day comes that his heart beats
    no more,
I'll bury my friend just beyond my back door.
And over his grave I'll post a big sign,
"Here lies Last Chance, a true friend of mine."

DAVID J. SANDERS

*("Last Chance" passed away in August of 1998 after
enjoying the last five years of his life with David and
his wife.)*

*Other Animals*

65

## The First of May

Now the smallest creatures, who do not know they
        have names,
In fields of pure sunshine open themselves and sing.
All over the marshes and in the wet meadows,
Wherever there is water, the companies of peepers
Who cannot count their members, gather with sweet
        shouting.
And the flowers of the woods who cannot see each
        other
Appear in perfect likeness of one another
Among the weak new shadows on the mossy places.
Now the smallest creatures, who know themselves by
        heart,
With all their tender might and roundness of delight
Spending their colors, their myriads and their voices
Praise the moist ground and every winking leaf,
And the new sun that smells of the new streams.

ANNE PORTER

*Other Animals*

## Midwife to Miracles

Knee-deep in dusty barnyard straw or snow on craggy hillsides, we sing your midwife praises, Loving Creator, as life renews itself in the cycle of your seasons. Piglets, smooth as velvet and pink as pearls; fuzzy lambs bleating with astonishment at finding themselves in my arms; calves all legs and nuzzling faces; and colts taking first steps, stumbling toward the milky prize. You've called us to tend them, blessing them as you bless us.

MARGARET ANNE HUFFMAN

*Other Animals*

## On Guardian Angels

Perhaps my angels have all along been birds.
How often am I out of their sight?
Even when I'm indoors, they come
to the window, seek me, keep watch.

So what if I can't understand their speech?
As long as the dawn hears the rooster and the waves
take their cue from the gulls, I too can have
their music without demanding sense of it.

In the main, my angels are small, brown sparrows,
who fly like tiny grapeshot & fastidiously watch,
but call little attention to themselves. They even
　　　seem
indifferent, but isn't that a perfect disguise?

RICHARD BEBAN

*Other Animals*

## In the Presence of Angels

I walked out alone in the evening and heard the birds singing in the full chorus of song, which can only be heard at that time of the year at dawn or at sunset. . . . A lark rose suddenly from the ground beside the tree by which I was standing and poured out its song above my head and then sank still singing to rest. Everything then grew still as the sunset faded and the veil of dusk began to cover the earth. I remember now the feeling of awe which came over me. I felt inclined to kneel to the ground, as though I had been standing in the presence of an angel; and I hardly dared to look on the face of the sky, because it seemed as though it was but a veil before the face of God.

BEDE GRIFFITHS

*Other Animals*

## Home Delivery

One local sparrow with chalky cheeks, rufous cap,
soft black beard commands the best magnolia twig,
trills the same song morning after morning.
Between notes he twists his head side to side,
scrapes conical beak back and forth against his
    perch,
as if on a razor strop. Some time ago I stopped
the morning paper; his sharp reports seem to be
all the news I need fresh out of sleep.

RICHARD BEBAN

*Other Animals*

*70*

## Bird Mother

Bird Mother,
You give me your song.
You give me your feathers.
You give me your sweet nectar.
You give me your nest in the eaves.

Bird Mother,
You greet me at the gate.
You show me the scaly pine's height.
You offer me the sky's vast freedom.
Now give me Your blessing, wherever I fly.

JANINE CANAN

*Other Animals*

71

## Birds Make Great Sky-Circles

Birds make great sky-circles
of their freedom.
How do they learn it?

They fall, and falling,
they're given wings.

RUMI
(1207–1273)
Translated by Coleman Barks, with John Moyne, A. J. Arberry, and
Reynold Nicholson

**Other Animals**

## The Communion of Saints

What I learned is that of all the creatures that I can see in this landscape, the geese best represent the communion of saints. They depend on one another. The lead goose does the most work, but when it is tired, it falls back and another takes its place. To be able to rely on others is a deep trust that does not come easily.

The geese fly in the wake of one another's wings. They literally get a lift from one another. I want to be with others this way. Geese tell me that it is, indeed, possible to fly with equals.

Gunilla Norris

*Other Animals*

## Deer Domain

As I wash the window
from inside,
I watch you
prodigally spend your way
through my yard.
You strip the arbor vita
as high as your teeth can reach,
mooch the dark green
of the lilac,
loot the tulips as they awaken.
When you lope toward the heart
of my Gold Dust hosta,
I want to rap on the glass
and stop you
from filching my garden trophy!
But, oh, the swagger
of your penny-colored back
the swing of your tawny neck
the flip of your white tail

*Other Animals*

your princely stance
remind me
that this was your dominion first
and I am the trespasser.

DONNA WAHLERT

*Other Animals*

## In Deer Country

Part leaf, part shade,
they stand beside the road,
and we are foreign. Out there
at the edge of the clearing,
some drift into the sun,
faces lowered to crop clover,
backs flecked with light.

In deer country, they live
in their own time; even running,
their limbs flow softly into grass,
their bodies weave like water.
They are the old way
of moving on the Earth.

PENNY HARTER

*Other Animals*

## The Grasshopper and the Cricket

The poetry of earth is never dead;
    When all the birds are faint with the hot sun,
    And hide in cooling trees, a voice will run
From hedge to hedge about the new-mown mead;
That is the Grasshopper's—he takes the lead
    In summer luxury,—he has never done
    With his delights; for when tired out with fun
He rests at ease beneath some pleasant weed.
The poetry of earth is ceasing never:
    On a lone winter evening, when the frost
      Has wrought a silence, from the stove there
        shrills
The Cricket's song, in warmth increasing ever,
    And seems to one in drowsiness half lost,
      The Grasshopper's among some grassy hills.

JOHN KEATS
(1795–1821)

*Other Animals*

## Atlantic Dolphins

Dolphins leap in the dawn,
their silver backs shedding
sparks of foam, their rhythm
a heartbeat beyond the breakers.

Welcoming the sun,
they raise salt into the wind
as they follow schools of fish
into the morning.

Tonight when they rest in the swells,
swimming with half-closed eyes,
blowholes open to the air,
they will listen for one another
and for the turning Earth
whose moon sounds the tides
that rock them;
                        and perhaps
they will dream of the stars,

**Other Animals**

pale phosphorescent ancestors
whistling faintly to them
from the distant currents
of the sky.

PENNY HARTER

*Other Animals*

## In a Moonlit Night

In a moonlit night on a spring day,
The croak of a frog
Pierces the whole cosmos and turns it into a single
     family!

WRITINGS OF CHANG CHIU-CHI'EN
Classical Zen Buddhist Poet

*Other Animals*

## Again, Frogs

Again, frogs courting.
First one starts, a violinist
trying his bow across the string,
then two or three more tune up.
Then a symphony, along the riverbank,
out of ponds. And the birds,
hidden in a thousand trees.

JUDITH MINTY

**Other Animals**

## Bee! I'm Expecting You!

Bee! I'm expecting you!
Was saying Yesterday
To Somebody you know
That you were due –

The Frogs got Home last Week –
Are settled, and at work –
Birds, mostly back –
The Clover warm and thick –

You'll get my Letter by
The seventeenth; Reply
Or better, be with me –
Yours, Fly.

EMILY DICKINSON
(1830–1886)

*Other Animals*

## The Good Life

Life in the barn was very good—night and day, winter and summer, spring and fall, dull days and bright days. It was the best place to be, thought Wilbur, this warm delicious cellar, with the garrulous geese, the changing seasons, the heat of the sun, the passage of swallows, the nearness of rats, the sameness of sheep, the love of spiders, the smell of manure, and the glory of everything.

E. B. WHITE
(1899–1985)
From *Charlotte's Web*

*Other Animals*

# Partings

## Time to Say Good-bye

As we lay our hands upon you,
Before your final rest,
Our hearts surround to love you,
And thank you for your best.
Our home you watched and treasured,
Our lives you truly blessed.

Lessening now your burdens,
We tend your tired bones.
Let us be your pillow,
Then wings to take you home.
Listen for God's calling,
Sweet promises of peace.
Old friend, leap to Heaven,
Suffering released!

ANNIE DOUGHERTY

*Partings*

## Mourning the Death of a Pet

There's nothing silly about the pain that follows the loss of a much-loved animal. . . .

Be prepared for the insensitive comments of others, such as "It was only a cat" or "Why don't you just get another bird?" Not everyone has had a friendship with an animal and can understand the sadness of losing it.

SUSAN LANDSMAN

*Partings*

## Long Lost . . . Long Remembered

*She's probably out having fun. Don't worry.*
But I did.
*She'll come back when she's hungry.*
But you didn't.
*Put an ad in the paper. That should work.*
But it didn't.
*A new pet will help.*
But it wasn't you.
*You should be over this by now.*
But I wasn't.
*You'll forget in time.*
But I never did.

I still miss you, and think of you often
And while I don't know where you are, or exactly
what happened
I can look at the stars on a crystal-clear night
And know
That you know
I cared.

JOANNA EMERY

**Partings**

## Prayer for a Pet's Memorial Service

God of all creatures, ease our grief today as we bid farewell to _____ (pet's name), whose passing leaves a gap in our family circle. She demanded so little of us—fresh water, food, a patch of sunlight for sunbathing, our presence—and gave so much in return—uncritical, undemanding, unlimited affection and devotion for all of us. Greeting each day, each moment, happily on its own terms, she showed us how to live in the present rather than regret the past or worry about the future. She wasn't perfect. She embarrassed herself with accidents and destroyed a few things, but we knew she never meant it maliciously. And her easy forgiveness of our flaws, her inability to hold a grudge, gave us an example of grace. Creator, we're grateful for being allowed to share her life for our allotted time. We will miss her bounding through our family life, but she will always be present in our hearts. Amen.

*Partings*

SUZANNE C. COLE

## Prayer for the Burial of a Bird

This sparrow died today, O Lord,
Your feathered creature small.
We lay him in the friendly earth
And ask Your blessing on us all.

ESTHER WILKEN

**Partings**

## Funeral Prayer

Note from the submitter, Maureen Tolman Flannery:

*When we were little girls on the sheep ranch, my sister and I were given orphan lambs to bottle-feed, and by the end of the summer they followed us around like the nursery rhyme. When two of our pet lambs died at the same time, it was a true family disaster complete with much weeping. We wrapped their bodies in blankets and carried them to the end of the horse pasture, where my father had prepared a joint grave. He had written this poem, which we continued to use, with only slight alteration, for the funerals of the many nursed and cared-for animals who needed funerals in the years to come. I then went on to use it for the interment of my children's pets and when we buried wild animals. My father is now eighty-five years old and continues to nurse every injured wild thing he encounters. Here is the prayer he wrote for his little girls' (about four and six years old) first personal encounter with death.*

Here lie two
little lambs of mine.
We lay them to rest
'neath the warm sunshine.
One was Dean,
and one Lulabelle.
They were good little lambs
and we loved them well.
But "from ashes to ashes,
from dust to dust,"
they were born into the world
and return they must.
So to heaven they go,
with all our love—
to romp and play
with God above.

DEAN TOLMAN

*Partings*

## Farewell, Old Friend

Thank you for your hand on the shovel, Lord, for it's nearly impossible to dig an old friend's grave through tears. As we lay him to rest, we feel his great spirit, healthy, whole, and spry once more, moseying contentedly along beloved paths. Our memories will always know we have been improved by our life together. Come next spring, there will be tender, lush grass, or perhaps a trailing flower or two, on the healing grave, spread as gently as only you and Mother Nature can do when given a little time—and friends' tears that fall like gentle, remembering rain.

MARGARET ANNE HUFFMAN

*Partings*

## An Epitaph

(Inscription on a monument at Newstead Abbey)

Near this spot
    Are deposited the remains of one
    Who possessed beauty without vanity,
    Strength without insolence,
    Courage without ferocity,
And all the virtues of man without his vices.

This praise, which would be unmeaning flattery
    If inscribed over human ashes,
    Is but a just tribute to the memory of
    Boatswain, a dog.

LORD BYRON
(1788–1824)

*Partings*

95

## Passing On

When a dog finally passes on, there is an emptiness, a place in our hearts that will never be filled again in exactly the way it was. Because no matter how many dogs we have over the years, each is unique, a friend, and when they go away, our lives are changed forever in many small ways.

STEVE SMITH

*Partings*

## At the Grave of a Fine Cat

May your whiskers be ruffled by only pleasant
    breezes,
May your bowls be filled with tuna and sweet cream,
May your dreams be blessed with legions of mice,
And most of all,
May you forever purr in peace.
Amen.

BARBARA YOUNGER

*Partings*

## A Memorial for a Pet

Dear God, Creator of all creatures great and small,

   We have lost our beloved pet and we gather today with sadness in our hearts. Yet we are here to celebrate the life of (pet's name). We remember the playful moments, the quiet moments, and the love we shared. These are the memories of our friend that we will treasure always. (You may ask each person to share a memory of the pet.) We thank you for the days we spent with (name), for pets everywhere, and for all of the wonderful creatures that you have placed upon our earth. Amen.

BARBARA YOUNGER

*Partings*

## In the Loss of Your Pet

There must be a heaven
for the animal friends we love.
They are not human,
yet they bring out
our own humanity . . .
sometimes in ways
that other people cannot.
They do not worry
about fame or fortune . . .
instead, they bring our hearts
nearer to the joy of simple things.
Each day they teach us
little lessons in trust
and steadfast affection.
Whatever heaven may be,
there's surely a place in it
for friends as good as these.

AUTHOR UNKNOWN

*Partings*

## A Dog Lover's Prayer

My prayer book's unconventional,
An album scarred with age.
The dogs who shared their lives with mine
Stand out on every page.

The spaniels of my childhood days,
All floppy ears and fluff;
The Dobermans who shared my bed,
Magnificent and tough.

Though some folks picture Heaven's gates
Atop a golden stair,
The precious photos in my book
Inspire this humble prayer:

Lord, lead me to a sun-washed field,
Then send them one by one;
Let yelps of joy lead wagging tails
As to my arms they run.

Sad eyes so pleading, paws that beg,
A symphony of barks

*Partings*

Invite a romp in fragrant grass
To songs of meadowlarks.

This Heaven that I pray for, Lord,
Where lilacs scent the air,
Is blessed with all the dogs I've loved
Who come to greet me there.

Toni Fulco

*Partings*

*101*

## Dogs in Heaven?

You think that these dogs will not be in Heaven! I tell you they will be there long before any of us.

ROBERT LOUIS STEVENSON
(1850–1894)

*Partings*

*102*

*Friends in the Great Beyond*

Do not weep for me when I am gone
For I have friends in the great beyond.
All the little ones I used to feed
Will come to me in my time of need.
They will purr and bark in great delight,
And I will hold and hug them tight.
Oh what a great day that will be
When my furry friends all welcome me.

RICHARD SEVERO

**Partings**

## The Love They Give Us

Not only is there always another good animal in need of a good home, but we must remember to be thankful for the time and love our animals give us while they are here. Take time to enjoy them and learn from them. As painful as it is to lose them, they teach us to love unselfishly, they teach us to live each day to the fullest, they teach us how to grow old gracefully, and they teach us how to die with dignity. We do them a disrespect to focus only on the sorrow of their death when they have given us so much joy through their life. If we wish to honor them, take what they have given us, all that love, and give it back to another animal in need of help.

KENT C. GREENOUGH

*Partings*

## Northwest Indian Memorial on Death

Do not stand at my grave and weep.
I am not there.
I do not sleep.
I am a thousand winds that blow.
I am the diamond glint on snow.
I am the sunlight on ripened grain.
I am the autumn rain.
When you awake in the morning hush,
I am the swift uplifting rush
Of birds circling in flight.
I am the stars that shine at night.
Do not stand at my grave and weep.
I am not there.
I do not sleep.

AUTHOR UNKNOWN

**Partings**

# FIVE

# Reflections

## If Having a Soul

If having a soul means being able to feel love and loyalty and gratitude, then animals are better off than a lot of humans.

JAMES HERRIOT
(1916–1995)

*Reflections*

## Do Animals Have Souls?

To me, animals have all the traits indicative of soul. For soul is not something we can see or measure. We can only observe its outward manifestations: in tears and laughter, in courage and heroism, in generosity and forgiveness. Soul is what's behind-the-scenes in the tough and tender moments when we are most intensely and grippingly alive. But what exactly is soul? Soul is the point at which our lives intersect the timeless, in our love of goodness, our zest for beauty, our passion for truth. Soul is what makes each of our lives a microcosm—not just a meaning-less fragment of the universe, but at some level a reflection of the whole.

No one can prove animals have souls. But if we open our hearts to other creatures and allow ourselves to sympathize with their joys and struggles, we find they have the power to touch and transform us. There is an inwardness in other creatures that awakens what is innermost in ourselves.

Reflections

For ages people have known that animals have a balance and harmony we can learn from. "Ask the beasts, and they will teach you," counsels the Book of Job.

Can we open our hearts to the animals? Can we greet them as our soul mates, beings like ourselves who possess dignity and depth? To do so, we must learn to revere and respect the creatures who, like us, are a part of God's beloved creation, and to cherish the amazing planet that sustains our mutual existence. We must join in a biospirituality that will acknowledge and celebrate the sacred in all life.

GARY KOWALSKI

*Reflections*

## They Shall Teach Thee

But ask now the beasts,
and they shall teach thee;
and the fowls of the air,
and they shall tell thee:
Or speak to the earth,
and it shall teach thee:
and the fishes of the sea
shall declare unto thee.

JOB 12:7–8 KJV

*Reflections*

## Ethical Conduct

By ethical conduct toward all creatures, we enter into
a spiritual relationship with the universe.

ALBERT SCHWEITZER
(1875–1965)

*Reflections*

*113*

## Love Animals

Love animals. God has given them the rudiments of thought and joy untroubled. Do not trouble their joy, do not harass them, do not deprive them of their happiness, do not work against God's intention.

FYODOR DOSTOYEVSKY
(1821–1881)
From *The Brothers Karamazov*

*Reflections*

## Hurt No Living Thing

Hurt no living thing;
>Ladybird, nor butterfly,
Nor moth with dusty wing,
>Nor cricket chirping cheerily;
Nor grasshopper so light of leap.
>Nor dancing gnat, nor beetle fat,
Nor harmless worms that creep.

CHRISTINA ROSSETTI
(1830–1894)

*Reflections*

## Moral Progress

The greatness of a nation and its moral progress can be judged by the way its animals are treated.

MOHANDAS GANDHI
(1869–1948)

*Reflections*

*116*

## Living Holy

I would give nothing
for that man's religion
whose very dog and cat
are not the better for it!

ROWLAND HILL
(1744–1833)

*Reflections*

## A True Perspective

In order to keep a true perspective of one's impor-
tance, everyone should have a dog that will worship
him and a cat that will ignore him.

DEREKE BRUCE

*Reflections*

*118*

## Animals Are Such Agreeable Friends

Animals are such agreeable friends—
they ask no questions,
they pass no criticisms . . .

GEORGE ELIOT
(1819–1880)

*Reflections*

## I Think I Could Turn and Live with the Animals

I think I could turn and live with the animals, they
are so placid and self-contain'd,

I stand and look at them long and long.

They do not sweat and whine about their condition,
They do not lie awake in the dark and weep for their
    sins.
They do not make me sick discussing their duty to
    God,
Not one is dissatisfied, not one is demented with the
    mania of owning things,
Not one kneels to another, nor to his kind that lived
    thousands of years ago,
Not one is respectable or unhappy over the whole
    earth.

WALT WHITMAN
(1819–1892)
From *Song of Myself*

*Reflections*

120

## To Portland Cement from Robert Frost

Whose woods these are
I think I know
They belong to the kingfisher, wren, and crow
They belong to the deer and the red-tailed hawk
That I see daily on my walk.
They belong to the great horned owl
And great blue heron,
Red fox, black mink,
And all their kin.
Don't turn them to condominium.
My big black Lab will think it queer
If there's a subdivision here.
What will become of all things wild
When there is black macadam piled,
When the stream is dry and the reed-lined pond
That the wild geese stop and settle on,
When the dead tree's gone, with its hollow nest
Where the pileated woodpecker used to rest
With its ivory bill and its flaming crest?

BARBARA CROOKER

**Reflections**

*121*

# Contemplation

If I spent enough time
with the tiniest creature—
even a caterpillar—
I would never have to
prepare a sermon. So full of
God is every creature.

MEISTER ECKHART
(1260–1327)

*Reflections*

## Child's Lesson

Teaching a child not to step on a caterpillar is as valuable to the child as it is to the caterpillar.

BRADLEY MILLER

*Reflections*

## Dream Time

*Australian Aboriginals say that their totemic ancestors walked across the land leaving words and musical notes in their footprints. They read the country as a musical score.*

In the Dream Time,
the Ancestors went underground,
Honey-Ant here, Wallaby there,
after their magic feet
had planted songs in the dust,

and by these songs, the people
learned each totem path,
singing the holy hillock, sacred spring,
and burning bush of their clan;
mapping kinship where the tongue shifted
but the song continued,
humming up from the underworld
like the first rivers.

When I listen to the whales
calling deep sea currents alive,
their repeating melodies answered

across great distances;
when I hear the wolves, the birds—
all the tribes descended from the Ancestors
learning the planet by ear,
defining it by song
as the wind does each tree,
I do what I can,
throwing this song out from my house
like a rope in search of water
through the fire.

PENNY HARTER

*Reflections*

## All Things Are Connected

What is man without the beasts? If all the beasts were gone, men would die from great loneliness of spirit, for whatever happens to the beasts also happens to man. All things are connected. Whatever befalls the earth befalls the children of the earth.

CHIEF SEATTLE
(1786–1866)

*Reflections*

## The Animals Never Yell at Me

The animals never yell at me.
The animals never make me do things
I don't want to do.
They don't expect too much of me.
They don't get mean or mad.
They're always there to run with me.
And make me feel not sad.

MICHAEL, AGE 10

*Reflections*

## An Animal's Eyes

An animal's eyes have the power to speak a great
language.

MARTIN BUBER
(1878–1965)

*Reflections*

## The Peace of Wild Things

When despair for the world grows in me
and I wake in the night at the least sound
in fear of what my life and my children's lives may be,
I go and lie down where the wood drake
rests in his beauty on the water, and the great heron
     feeds.
I come into the peace of wild things
who do not tax their lives with forethought
of grief. I come into the presence of still water.
And I feel above me the day-blind stars
waiting with their light. For a time
I rest in the grace of the world, and am free.

WENDELL BERRY

*Reflections*

## If I Knew the Ways of Animals

If I knew the sweep of winged things
—the sulphur among the alfalfas
the lark in the sky—
I would know everything
the eagle knows
about the earth's fine geometry
and its handsome curvature

If I knew the compass of creeping, crawling things
—the worm that comes out to greet the rain
the caterpillar that has its cheek on beauty—
I would know everything
the garter snake knows
about mixing colors
to match the palette of mottled leaves
that have fallen from the paper birch

If I knew the ways of majestic beasts
—the lion's proud strutting
the elephant's lumbering walk—
I would know everything
the wolf knows

*Reflections*

which has left
a scattering of feathers
that belonged to a grouse

If I knew the sail that belonged to swift things
—the cheetah's explosive dash
the quick scamper of a squirrel to the tree top—
I would know everything
the gazelle knows
the way he walks
among the sounds of the forest

If I knew the habits of near-home creatures
—the owl in its bower
the cat at the window sunning himself—
and could meditate on the grandeur that marks the
     land
I would know everything
a good heart knows
the voice of God from his resplendent tower.

S. RAMNATH

*Reflections*

*131*

## God's Special Providence

The insect in the plant, the moth which spends its brief hours of existence hovering about the candle's flame—nay, the life which inhabits a drop of water, is as much an object of God's special providence as the mightiest monarch on his throne.

HENRY BERGH
Founder, American Society for the Prevention of Cruelty to Animals

*Reflections*

## God in All Things

Apprehend God in all things,
for God is in all things.
Every single creature is full of God
and is a book about God.
Every creature is a word of God.

MEISTER ECKHART
(1260–1327)

*Reflections*

## Talk to the Animals

If you talk to the
animals, they will
talk to you.
And you will know
each other.
If you do not talk to the
animals, you will
not know them.
And what you do not
know, you will fear.
What one fears, one
destroys.

CHIEF DAN GEORGE

*Reflections*

*134*

## In Their Innocence and Wisdom

In their innocence and wisdom, in their connection
to the earth and its most ancient rhythms, animals
show us a way back to a home they have never left.

SUSAN CHERNAK MCELROY
From *Animals as Teachers and Healers*

*Reflections*

*135*

## Prayer for an Ill Pet

Our heavenly Creator, who knows and cares for the smallest sparrow, we ask your blessing for our dear companion who now lies ill. Yet even in pain and discomfort, our pet is concerned for us, trying valiantly to cheer us with the touch of an encouraging paw. We would ask that _____ (pet's name) be made strong and healthy again to return to the center of our family life. If this is not possible, then we ask that our pet, who is unable to understand why it hurts and unable to tell us where it hurts, be released from suffering. We pray for the grace to be unselfish enough to let him go. Amen.

SuzAnne C. Cole

*Reflections*

## To Be of Service

Not to hurt our humble brethren is our first duty to them, but to stop there is not enough. We have a higher mission—to be of service to them wherever they require it.

SAINT FRANCIS OF ASSISI
(1181–1226)

*Reflections*

## Why Do I Care So Much?

Even if all research labs could be redesigned to
provide the best possible environment for the chimpanzee subjects, there would still be one nagging
question—should chimpanzees be used at all? Are
we really justified in putting our closest relatives in
the animal kingdom into cages and subjecting them
to lives of slavery for the sake of human health? Just
because we have decided that it is not ethical to use
human "guinea pigs"? We have far more in common
with chimpanzees than the physiological characteris-
tics that make them, in the eyes of some scientists, so
suitable for certain kinds of research. We should not
forget that there are equally striking similarities in
the social behavior, intellect, and emotions of human
beings and chimpanzee beings. And I personally
believe that if we have souls, then probably chimpanzees have them too. . . .

Why do I care so much? Why, in order to try to
change attitudes and actions in the labs, do I subject
myself repeatedly to the personal nightmare of visit-
ing these places, knowing that I shall be haunted

endlessly by memories of my encounters with the prisoners there? Especially their eyes, those bewildered or sad or angry eyes. The answer is simple. I have spent so many years in the forests of Gombe, being with and learning from the chimpanzees. I consider myself one of the luckiest people on earth. It is time to repay something of the old debt I owe the chimpanzees, for what they have taught me about themselves, about myself, about the place of humans and chimpanzees in the natural world.

JANE GOODALL
(Two million chimpanzees lived in the wild in 1900; fewer than 150,000 remain today.)

*Reflections*

## Compassion

[Concern for animals] is a matter of taking the side of the weak against the strong, something the best people have always done.

HARRIET BEECHER STOWE
(1811–1896)

*Reflections*

## Until One Has Loved an Animal

Until one has loved an animal, a part of one's soul remains unawakened.

ANATOLE FRANCE
(1844–1924)

**Reflections**

## We All Belong to the Same Family

We are part of the earth and it is part of us. The perfumed flowers are our sisters; the deer, the horse, the great eagle, these are our brothers. The rocky crests, the juices of the meadows, the body heat of the pony, and man—all belong to the same family.

CHIEF SEATTLE
(1786–1866)

*Reflections*

## Respect for Life

Any religion not based on respect for life
is not a true religion.

Until he extends his circle of compassion
to all living things,
man will not himself find peace.

ALBERT SCHWEITZER
(1875–1965)

*Reflections*

## All Things Bright and Beautiful

All things bright and beautiful,
All creatures great and small,
All things wise and wonderful,
The Lord God made them all.

Each little flower that opens,
Each little bird that sings,
He made their flowing colours,
He made their tiny wings.

He gave us eyes to see them,
And lips that we might tell,
How great is God Almighty,
Who has made all things well.

CECIL FRANCES ALEXANDER
(1818–1895)

*Reflections*

*144*

# SIX

# Inspiration

# A Prayer for the Feast of St. Francis

Remember, in our prayers today
All creatures wild or tame;
Exotic, unfamiliar ones
And household pets you call by name;
The bold, the shy, the slow or swift,
The ones with teeth and claws,
The ones with scales or shells or fins,
The ones with hooves or paws;
The shaggy-maned, the silken-furred,
The winged and feathered of the skies,
All those with antler, horn, or tusk,
All those with gentle eyes;
The caged, the free, the ones who toil,
The ones who crawl or swim or sting,
The ones most loved, the ones most feared,
The ones who howl or buzz or sing;
All dwellers of the sea or plain,
Of desert, mountain, jungle, farm;
Pray for the creatures of the earth
To keep them safe from harm.

SHEILA FORSYTH

Inspiration

## Animal Blessing for the Feast of St. Francis of Assisi

O God, source of all life and energy, You who created
    the animals
because your universe was incomplete without them,
Bless these loving creatures that we bring before You
    today.

Bless these cats and dogs and mammals who amble
    through your grasses;
Bless these birds that wing the rich air that You
    breathe forth;
Bless these fish that dart through the living waters
    that You provide;
And these snakes that slither with a kind agenda.
Protect all of them from harm and their own
    curiosities.

*Inspiration*

148

Bless the caretakers of these animal companions;
Nourish them so that they may reflect the simplicity,
    honesty,
and unconditional love of these pets. Mindful of your
    desire

for harmony and wholeness within all of your
    creation,
and inspired by St. Francis, we ask these things with
    humble faith.

DONNA WAHLERT

*Inspiration*

## A Prayer for a Pet Blessing

O Creator of Companions,

At this Pet Blessing, we are reminded that relationships of love and justice with the animals that share our lives extend our relations with You. Your ideal of the peaceable kingdom, of the lion lying with the lamb and the child playing over the snake's den, requires both beasts and humans.

We know You love animals because You made them. You do not forget them. You notice the falling sparrow, You clothe the lilies of the field and feed and shelter the birds of the air. These are signs of Your love for them—and for us, Your creatures, too.

By bringing us together—man and beast—to love one another, You offer peace. Our human act of blessing the animals simply returns thanks to You for blessing us through them.

Thank you, God.

MARTHA K. BAKER

*Inspiration*

## A Prayer for Animals

O God, we thank thee
for all the creatures thou hast made,
so perfect in their kind—
great animals like the elephant and the rhinoceros,
humorous animals like the camel and the monkey,
friendly ones like the dog and the cat,
working ones like the horse and the ox,
timid ones like the squirrel and the rabbit,
majestic ones like the lion and the tiger,
for birds with their songs.
O God, give us such love for thy creation,
that love may cast out fear,
and all thy creatures—and thy creation—
see in men and women like us
their priest and their friend. . . .

GEORGE APPLETON

*Inspiration*

*151*

## I Sing for the Animals

Out of the earth
I sing for them,
A Horse nation
I sing for them.
Out of the earth
I sing for them,
The animals
I sing for them.

TETON SIOUX INDIANS

*Inspiration*

*152*

## A Prayer for Protecting Animals

O God, source of life and power, Who feedeth the birds of the heavens, increase our tenderness towards all the creatures of Thy hand. Help us to refrain from petty acts of cruelty, or thoughtless deeds of harm to any living animal. May we care for them at all times, especially during hard weather, and protect them from injury so that they learn to trust us as friends. Let our sympathy grow with knowledge, so that the whole creation may rejoice in Thy presence.

AUTHOR UNKNOWN

*Inspiration*

*Blessings*

Lord, thank you for blessing our lives with animals.
Tender of heart and pure in soul,
They touch us in so many ways.
Commitment, unconditional love, faith, and
      forgiveness,
Inherent traits never questioned nor compromised,
Yet shared and bequeathed freely
Upon any and all who offer them the same.
It is with animals that we are taught tolerance and
      diversity,
For their uniqueness serves to brighten our existence.
They are an incomparable gift from God,
One that we open and rediscover daily,
Showing us how to make the world a little better,
And our society a bit more humane.
Lord, thank you for blessing our lives with animals.
For it is within these divine creatures that we
      rediscover
The true meanings of your teachings and infinite
      wisdom.

HEATHER BERRY

*Inspiration*

154

*Buddhist Prayer*

May every creature abound in well-being and peace.
May every living being, weak or strong, the long and
      the small,
The short and the medium-sized, the mean and the
      great,
May every living being, seen or unseen, those
      dwelling far off,
Those nearby, those already born, those waiting to be
      born,
May all attain inward peace.

AUTHOR UNKNOWN

*Inspiration*

## A Blessing for a Child's New Pet

May this little pet bring pleasure and make
   the cloudiest days seem bright
May this little pet bring comfort and warmth
   when the world feels cold and lonely
May this little pet teach patience and caring—
   the foundation of all earthly peace
May this little pet foster understanding through
   the universal language of life and love
May this little pet grow along with this child
   from season to season and year to year
May this little pet create love everywhere through
   its sheer being in our lives

JOANNA EMERY

*Inspiration*

## In Appreciation of the Family Pet

They love without strings attached, these loving beasts of your hand, O God of amazing critters. Bless them, for they bless us even when they leave muddy paw prints on clean floors, ignore our commands, and shed on the furniture. Keep us worthy of their trust.

MARGARET ANNE HUFFMAN

*Inspiration*

*157*

## Rainforest Life

In the trees
Far above,
Live the creatures
Of this forest.
Fragile canopies protect them,
Natural growth feeds them.
Life sustains life
In this tropical wilderness.

May the forces of civilization,
with its fire and
Machines of destruction
Be still,
So the chirping,
And swinging,
Crawling, and singing,
Last forever.

Amen.

PAULA E. KIRMAN

*Inspiration*

## Blessings in All Directions

We look to the north and see
hardy caribou, noble elk
the husky, rolling in snow
the salmon struggling upstream to spawn
the deer whisking his tail with elegance.

We look to the south and watch
the alligator measuring the pond
the armadillo turning his armor to the world
the wings of pelican, wood stork, heron
catching the low warm air streams.

To the west is the
rim-eyed panda, the yak, the kiwi,
a koala nestled in the fork of a blue gum tree
the take-charge kangaroo and wallaby
leaping to attention, balancing the world on
    thick tails.

The red earth of the east
is the setting for the stately parade
of giraffe, elephant, gazelle,

*Inspiration*

159

fringed lion, svelte tiger, portly hippo—
all staking a claim for their home on the continent.

We look nearer to home and glimpse
the curious Persian cat, the faithful Labrador,
the regal quarter horse
content goldfish, clever hamsters,
the reptile appreciating friendship.

As we finish taking inventory,
We send up a prayer of thanksgiving
for these blest animals, who reflect all of creation,
and who share with us
this air
this water
this dust.

DONNA WAHLERT

*Inspiration*

*Hear Our Humble Prayer*

Hear our humble prayer, O God, for our friends the animals, especially for animals who are suffering; for any that are hunted or lost or deserted or frightened or hungry; for all that must be put to death. We entreat for them all Thy mercy and pity, and for those who deal with them we ask a heart of compassion and gentle hands, and kindly words. Make us, ourselves, to be true friends to animals and so to share the blessing of the merciful.

AUTHOR UNKNOWN

*Inspiration*

# Author Index

*Author Index*

# Permissions and Acknowledgments

*Grateful acknowledgment is made to the authors and publishers for the use of the following material. Every effort has been made to contact original sources. If notified, the publishers will be pleased to rectify an omission in future editions.*

Martha K. Baker for "A Prayer for a Pet Blessing."

Coleman Barks for "Birds Make Great Sky-Circles" by Jalal Al-Din Rumi from *The Essential Rumi*, translated by Coleman Barks, published by Harper SanFrancisco. Copyright ©1995 by Coleman Barks. Reprinted by kind permission of Coleman Barks.

Richard Beban for "Home Delivery," "On Guardian Angels," and "Time Spent Watching a Cat."

Heather Berry for "Blessings."

Wendell Berry for "The Peace of Wild Things" excerpted from *Openings* by Wendell Berry.

Copyright ©1968 by Wendell Berry. Published by Harcourt Brace. Reprinted with permission of the author.

Janine Canan for "Bird Mother."

SuzAnne C. Cole for "Prayer for a Pet's Memorial Service" and "Prayer for an Ill Pet."

Barbara Crooker for "To Portland Cement from Robert Frost."

Crown Publishing Group for "The Communion of Saints" from *Journeying in Place* by Gunilla Norris. Copyright ©1994 by Gunilla Norris. Reprinted by kind permission of The Crown Publishing Group.

Mary Maude Daniels for "Companion" and "Peace Keeper."

Doris Day for "Comfort."

Annie Dougherty for "Time to Say Good-bye."

Joanna Emery for "A Blessing For a Child's First Pet," and "Long Lost . . . Long Remembered."

Susan J. Erickson for "Psalm for a Cat Owner."

Ida Fasel for "Passerby."

Maureen Tolman Flannery for "Funeral Prayer."

Sheila Forsyth for "A Prayer for the Feast of St. Francis."

Katy Friends for "Faithful Companion."

Toni Fulco for "A Dog Lover's Prayer."

Golden Book Publishing Co. for "Prayer for the Burial of a Bird" from *The Golden Books Treasury of Prayers from Around the World* by Esther Wilkin. Copyright ©1975 by Esther Wilkin. Reprinted by permission of Golden Book Publishing Co.

Kent C. Greenough for "The Love They Give Us."

Harcourt, Inc. for "The King of Cats Sends a Postcard to His Wife" from *A Visit to William Blake's Inn* by Nancy Willard. Copyright ©1981 by Nancy Willard. Reprinted by permission of Harcourt, Inc.

Harvard University Press for "Bee! I'm Expecting You" by Emily Dickinson. Reprinted by permission of the publishers and the Trustees of Amherst College from *The Poems of Emily Dickinson*, Thomas H. Johnson, ed., Cambridge, Mass.: The Belknap Press of Harvard University Press. Copyright © 1951, 1955, 1979 by the President and Fellows of Harvard College.

The Harvill Press of London and Templegate Publishers of Springfield, Illinois for "In the Presence of Angels" by Bede Griffiths from *The Golden String*. First published in Great Britain in 1980 by Harvill. Copyright ©1980 by Bede Griffiths. Reproduced by permission of the Bede Griffiths Trust, The Harvill Press, and Templegate Publishers.

Houghton Mifflin Company for excerpts from *Visions of Caliban*. Copyright ©1993 by Dale Peterson and Jane Goodall. Reprinted by permission of Houghton Mifflin Company. All rights reserved.

Kathleen McKinley Harris for "Cat from the Animal Shelter."

Penny Harter for "Atlantic Dolphins," "Dream Time," and "In Deer Country."

C. David Hay for "Old Friends."

Margaret Anne Huffman for "Farewell, Old Friend;" "In Appreciation of the Family Pet;" "Midwife to Miracles;" "Room for One More;" and "Welcome Home, New Puppy."

Nicolas Kallistos for "A Fieldmouse's Prayer."

Paula E. Kirman for "Rainforest Life."

Arlene Gay Levine for "Magician."

Janet McCann for "I Would Be."

Susan Chernak McElroy for "In Their Innocence and Wisdom" from *Animals as Teachers and Healers* by Susan Chernak McElroy. Copyright ©1997 by Susan Chernak McElroy. Reprinted by permission of Susan Chernak McElroy.

Rhena Schweitzer Miller for "Ethical Conduct" and "Respect for Life" by Albert Schweitzer. Reprinted by kind permission of Rhena Schweitzer Miller.

Judith Minty for "Again, Frogs."

Cheryl Morikawa for "Three Little Fish."

Julia Older for "Old Black Lab in the First Snow."

Oxford University Press for "A Prayer for Animals" by George Appleton. Copyright ©1985 by George Appleton. Reprinted by permission of Oxford University Press.

Jenny-Marie Pulliam for "All God's Creatures."

S. Ramnath for "If I Knew the Ways of Animals."

Thomas L. Reid for "The Cat."

David J. Sanders for "Last Chance."

Scribner, a Division of Simon & Schuster, for "Cats as Teachers" from *Spiritual Literacy* by Frederic and Mary Ann Brussat. Copyright ©1996 by Frederic and Mary Ann Brussat. Reprinted by permission of Scribner, a Division of Simon & Schuster.

Stillpoint Press for "Do Animals Have Souls?" from *The Souls of Animals* by Gary Kowalski, Copyright ©1991 by Stillpoint Press. Reprinted by kind permission of Stillpoint Publishing.

Dean Tolman for "Funeral Prayer."

Ÿ. Max Valentonis for "Cat-Haiku-Esque-Poem."

Donna Wahlert for "Animal Blessing for the Feast of St. Francis of Assisi," "Blessings in All Directions," and "Deer Domain."

Willow Creek Press for "Passing On" from *Just Mutts* by Steve Smith. Copyright ©1999 Willow Creek Press. Reprinted by kind permission of Willow Creek Press.

Barbara Younger for "A Memorial for a Pet" and "At the Grave of a Fine Cat."

Zoland Books for "The First of May" from *An Altogether Different Language: Poems 1934–1994* by Anne Porter. Copyright ©1994 by Zoland Books. Reprinted by permission of Zoland Books.

*Permissions compiled by Rebecca Pirtle.*

**Permissions and Acknowledgments**

# Photo Credits

*Grateful acknowledgement is given to the following individuals for the photographs that appear in this book.*

Title page: "Cali and Peaches" from the author's private collection; Dedication page: "June with Thunder," "June with Sundance," and "June with Shalimar and Sundance" from the author's private collection; Dogs: "Bonnie" © Linda Woods; Cats: "Chester" © Mary Maude Daniels; Other Animals: "Showdown and Sure 'Nuf' a Winner" © Katharine Patricia Wilson; Partings: "Maya" © H. Michael Leavitt; Reflections: "Jamaica" © Hal Bush; Inspiration: "Daisy Mae" © Jerome Johnson. Endpaper montage: "Sundancer" © Cheryl A. Crain; "Wild deer" and "Thunder and Mary" from the author's private collection; "Chip" © Mary Maude Daniels; "Maggie" © Matthew Delaney; "Whiskers, Popeye, and Wilbur" and "Lucky" © Kris Ediger; "Sampson" © David Hennessy; "Blue Sky Lucky Seven" and "Blue Sky Miss Dolly" © Sirona Knight; "Sammy" © Lou Kurdziel; "Polly" © Terri Leonard; "Harry" © Jim Warner; "Mr. Cat" © Neil Cannon.